A WAY TO THE HEART OF
CHRISTMAS

A WAY TO THE HEART OF
CHRISTMAS

edited by
Brian Linard

illustrations by
Denise Silva

New City Press

Published in the United States by New City Press
202 Cardinal Rd., Hyde Park, NY 12538
©1991 New City Press

Text selections based on
They Laid Him in a Manger
©1990 New City, London, Great Britain

Cover painting by Lois Irsara

Library of Congress Cataloging-in-Publication Data:

A Way to the Heart of Christmas / Brian Linard, ed.

    Rev. ed. of: They laid Him in a manger. ©1990.
    Includes index.
    ISBN 1-56548-025-2 : $6.95
    1. Christmas—Meditation. 2. Christmas—Poetry. I. Linard,
    Brian. II. They laid Him in a manger.
    BV45.W33   1991
    242'.33—dc20   91-24362

1st printing: August 1991
3d printing: August 1994

Printed in the United States of America

CONTENTS

Foreword

A noted poet was once asked in an interview if he could explain one of his poems "in ordinary terms." He replied with some feeling: "If I could say what I meant in ordinary terms I would not have had to write the poem."

From the time of Christ's birth, the people of God have "had to write a poem" to Christmas, composing a single multi-stranded paean of praise spanning the centuries, because ultimately the meaning of Christmas resists being fully spelled out "in ordinary terms." Some of these strands recur constantly, albeit with infinitely varied nuances, becoming as familiar and necessary to the whole as a rhythm. One such is the ever-incredible paradox of the powerless Almighty—as, for instance, in the words of Hilary, Bishop of Poitiers: "We hear the one at whose word the angels and archangels tremble, cry like a child." Others speak of the infinite mercy of God, or hope renewed, or the motherhood of Mary. Still other strands, instead, seem to startle us with a flash of intuition, suddenly casting a new light on what we already know: "God became human that we might become human" (St. Augustine). And through all the strands runs a joyful refrain giving tongue to our deep-seated need to worship: "God's Son became a human being. All our efforts to understand this great mystery are in vain. All that we can do is what the shepherds did—worship, believe and praise God" (Cardinal Alfred Bengsch).

No one who has been exposed to any part of this sublime mystery can fail to be affected by it. And yet, so often a gnawing doubt assails us: our "real" Christmases, the ones we celebrate with decorated trees and presents, seem to be lived out under the sway of two very different—and yet related—realms. One is the realm of suffering: all that public and private anguish, loneliness and destruction that appear to be irreversibly cut off from the "good cheer" of the season—which seems in fact only to deepen the sense of despair for those unfortunate enough to be caught "on the outside" of Christmas; the other is the realm of Mammon, which seems to have appropriated Christmas for itself, retaining all the appearances of pious sentiment, of light and color (and, of course, the essential exchanging of gifts), while emptying it of all else—and in the process, compounding the loneliness and despair "outside."

How, we wonder, can the devout beliefs and practices of a simpler age hold out against such a harsh "reality"?

"God's becoming human is not an idyll. It is a scandal! God meets us in the lowliness of a child" (Klaus Hemmerle, Bishop of Aachen, Germany). This, then, is reality—it is precisely the suffering world, desperately in need of redemption, that cried out for God to come; God answered unexpectedly by becoming a baby destined to be martyred. The Christmas of Mammon, on the other hand, is an illusion that we are called to penetrate and reclaim for reality: "God became human. We did not become God. The human dispensation continues and it must continue. But it is consecrated. And we have become more. We have also been strengthened. Let us trust our life, then, because this night has brought us light. Let us trust life, because we do not live it alone. God lives it with us" (Alfred Delp, S.J., while awaiting execution by the Nazis).

This book is an attempt to expose us a little more to that light, to help us "trust our life" more than the illusions, by offering an almost random glimpse of a few of the strands of this awe-inspired symphony raised up by a grateful people which, aware that God now lives with us, "had to write a poem."

Brian Linard

In the beginning was the Word
the Word was in God's presence,
and the Word was God.
He was present to God in the beginning.
Through him all things came into being,
and apart from him nothing came to be.
Whatever came to be in him found life
life for the light of men.
The light shines on in darkness,
a darkness that did not overcome it.
The real light
which gives light to every man
was coming into the world.
He was in the world,
and through him the world was made,
yet the world did not know who he was.
To his own he came,
yet his own did not accept him.
Any who did accept him
he empowered to become children of God.
These are they who believe in his name—
who were begotten not by blood,
nor by carnal desire,
nor by man's willing it,
but of God.
The Word became flesh
and made his dwelling among us,
and we have seen his glory:
the glory of an only Son

coming from the Father,
filled with enduring love.

John 1:1-5, 9-14

"In the beginning was the Word." That's how St. John begins his gospel, his story of Good News. That Word, as you know, is Jesus Christ, the Son of God, who dwells among us, filled with God's enduring love.

There are no greater words than the Word that God speaks to us. There is no greater power on earth than God's Word. This Word is filled with unlimited love, care, and concern for each of us. That's the true meaning of Christmas: we celebrate because God loves us.

In the most basic sense, Christmas never changes. Over the centuries, despite the many traditions we have added to this day, the central fact remains: God almighty, the eternal One, creator of heaven and earth, becomes human. He comes to us in his Son, Jesus, a tiny infant—poor, humble, cared for by two simple people who are rich in nothing but faith and love. That is the unchanging picture of Christmas: the holy family surrounding the infant Jesus, God become human. Artists will never tire of portraying it. And who can resist being moved by it?

Joseph Cardinal Bernardin

The drama of human freedom is at the heart of the Prologue to John's Gospel. It is concerned with us, our everyday life and the decisions which we, in our freedom, are called to make. Christmas confronts us with the unlimited possibility of salvation that was revealed to us when the word of God entered our human history. What Saint John is telling us is that this possibility does not become a reality just of its own accord. It is an offer made to us in our freedom, something that we can either reject or accept. Celebrating the feast of Christmas means making room for the Lord who is coming.

Carlo Maria Martini
(Archbishop of Milan, b. 1927)

And the Word became flesh
and dwelt among us.
God's Word became human
to accustom human beings
to receiving God.
God had begun
to live with the human race.

Irenaeus
(Bishop of Lyons, Second Century)

With the fullness of time he appeared—the one who wanted to set us free from time. For, set free from time, we would be able to reach that eternity which is beyond time. We would therefore no longer need to say: When will the hour come? For it would be an eternal day. No yesterday would precede it and no tomorrow would follow it.

In this world, however, days go by and others come. No day remains. Even as we speak, the moments pass, the first syllable pressed on by the second that is waiting impatiently to be heard. As soon as we have spoken, we have become a little older. I am certainly older now than I was this morning. Nothing stands still. Nothing remains firm in time. We must therefore love the one through whom the times came to be, so that we may be set free from time and become established in eternity, where time and the changes it brings no longer exist.

It is, then, a great mercy on the part of our Lord Jesus Christ that he, through whom the times came to be, came to be for our sakes in time, that he, through whom all things came to be, came to be in the midst of all things, that he became what he had made. For he became what he had made. He, who had made the human race, became human, so that what he had made would not be lost.

Augustine
(Bishop of Hippo, d. 430)

The Word became flesh.
The Word became heart.
God accepted a heart.
God's heart beats
in the countless millions
of human hearts.
Since then we are able to know
what dwells in the heart of humanity,
because God who knows everything
wanted to be close to everything.
Not only did he want to know
what is in the heart of humanity—
he also wanted to experience it.
What is in our heart
may be troubled and disturbed,
but there is in it always a longing
for the answer "yes"—
"Don't write me off!"—"Forgive me!"—
"Give me another chance!"—"Accept me!"
And there is even more than this in every heart—
an even deeper mystery.
It is not just a longing—it is reality.
Every heart is a heart that is loved.
For every human heart
is worth God's won heart
and God has offered himself up
for every human being.

Klaus Hemmerle
(Bishop of Aachen, Germany)

16

In those days Caesar Augustus published a decree ordering a census of the whole world. This first census took place while Quirinius was governor of Syria. Everyone went to register, each to his own town. And so Joseph went from the town of Nazareth in Galilee to Judea, to David's town of Bethlehem—because he was of the house and lineage of David—to register with Mary, his espoused wife, who was with child.

While they were there the days of her confinement were completed. She gave birth to her first-born son and wrapped him in swaddling clothes and laid him in a manger, because there was no room for them in the place where travelers lodged.

There were shepherds in that region, living in the fields and keeping night watch by turns over their flocks. The angel of the Lord appeared to them as the glory of the Lord shone around them, and they were very much afraid. The angel said to them: "You have nothing to fear! I come to proclaim good news to you—tidings of great joy to be shared by the whole people. This day in David's city a savior has been born to you, the Messiah and Lord. Let this be a sign to you: in a manger you will find an infant wrapped in swaddling clothes." Suddenly, there was with the angel a multitude of the heavenly hosts, praising God and saying,

"Glory to God in high heaven,
peace on earth to those on whom
his favor rests."

When the angels had returned to heaven, the shepherds said to one another: "Let us go over to Bethlehem and see this event which the Lord has made known to us." They went in haste and found Mary and Joseph, and the baby lying in the manger; once they saw, they understood what had been told them concerning this child. All who heard of it were astonished at the report given them by the shepherds.

Mary treasured all these things and reflected on them in her heart. The shepherds returned, glorifying and praising God for all they had heard and seen, in accord with what had been told them.

Luke 2:1-20

He became a child
so that you could become a full mature
  human being.
He was wrapped in swaddling cloths
so that you could be unravelled
from the meshes of death.
He came on earth
so that you could live beneath the stars.
There was no place for him in the inn
so that there could be many dwelling places
for you in heaven.
He was rich,
but he became poor for us.
His poverty is our riches
and his weakness is our strength.
He is poor for us,
but in himself he is rich.
You can see him
lying there in swaddling cloths,
but what you cannot see
is that he is God's Son.

Ambrose
(Bishop of Milan, d.397)

Jesus came into this world, but he did not tell anyone, even those who were closest to him, who he was. If he had entered the world in his home in Nazareth, his coming might have been celebrated with great rejoicing by all his relatives and by the neighbors and all those who lived in the town. But he was born on a journey and in the midst of a great number of unknown people. So he really does belong to everyone—and he came very reticently, making no noise. There is no doubt God might have been able to do much more to spread the news of his coming, but it is clear that he does not want to thrust his Son upon us. He wants us to come to him. We have to look for him. We have to discover him. Yes, Jesus is infinitely reticent. He waits.

All the historical events surrounding Jesus' birth in Bethlehem at the turn of the age proclaim God in the silence of words. They were prophetic events speaking in silence to all the generations that have followed. But they are not in any way insistent, demanding to be understood at once. Jesus is patient. He has time.

René Voillaume
(Founder of the Little Brothers of Jesus)

In Bethlehem on a Christmas night
All around the Child shone a holy light.
All around His head was a halo bright
On a Christmas night.

"We have no room," the innkeeper called,
So the glory fell where the cows were stalled,
But among the guests were Three Kings who
  called
On a Christmas night.

How can it be such a light shines here
In this humble stable once cold and drear?
Oh, the Child has come to bring good cheer
On a Christmas night!

And what is the name of the little One?
His name is Jesus—He's God's own Son.
Be happy, happy, everyone
On a Christmas night!

Langston Hughes

This day to you a child is born
of maiden, chosen from all time.
A child so tender and so fine
should be your joy this Christmas morn.

He's Christ our Lord, our God who reigns.
He longs to save us from our woe,
his saving task to undergo
and wash us clean from sin and strain.

Praise be to God enthroned on high,
who sends his own beloved Son,
while angels sing in unison—
"a glad New Year" their joyful cry.

He brings you all great happiness,
prepared by God our Father's love,
that we with him in heaven above
may live in everlasting bliss.

Ah Lord, who madest all from clay,
how couldst thou be so small and poor,
to lie there in the dusty straw
where ox and ass feed every day?

Martin Luther
(1483-1546)

I sing the birth was born to-night,
The author both of life and light;
The angels so did sound it,
And, like the ravished shepherds said,
Who saw the light, and were afraid,
Yet searched, and true they found it.

The Son of God, the eternal king,
That did us all salvation bring,
And freed our soul from danger,
He whom the whole world could not take,
The Word, which heaven and earth did make,
Was now laid in a manger.

The Father's wisdom willed it so,
The Son's obedience knew no "No;"
Both wills were in one stature,
And, as that wisdom had decreed,
The Word was now made flesh indeed,
And took on Him our nature.

What comfort by Him we do win,
Who made Himself the price of sin,
To make us heirs of glory!
To see this babe, all innocence,
A martyr born in our defence,
Can man forget the story?

Ben Jonson
(1572-1637)

Out to the hillside to a stable cave, where shepherds sometimes drove their flocks in time of storm, Joseph and Mary went at last for shelter. There, in a place of peace in the lonely abandonment of a cold windswept cave; there, under the floor of the world, He Who is born without a mother in heaven, is born without a father on earth.

Of every other child that is born into the world, friends can say that it resembles his mother. This was the first instance in time that anyone could say that the mother resembled the child. This is the beautiful paradox of the child who made His mother; the mother, too, was only a child. It was also the first time in the history of this world that anyone could ever think of heaven as being anywhere else than "somewhere up there"; when the child was in her arms, Mary now looked down to Heaven.

Fulton J. Sheen

I stand here by your manger bed,
O Jesus, life to me!
I bring no gift but what instead
you gave me lovingly.
Take it—it is my mind and soul,
my heart, my spirit, courage, all!
And may it give you pleasure.

For long before I came to be,
you came with saving grace
to choose me from eternity
before I knew your face.
Even before your molding hand
had fashioned me, your love had planned how
you would shape my future.

I look at you with heartfelt joy
and cannot gaze my fill.
I know no better way to employ
my time than standing still.
O that my mind were an abyss,
my soul an ocean fathomless—
that I might comprehend you!

Paul Gerhardt
(1607-1676)

Lord! When thou didst thy selfe undresse
Laying by thy robes of glory,
To make us more, thou wouldst be lesse,
And becam'st a wofull story.

To put on Clouds instead of light,
And cloath the morning-starre with dust,
Was a translation of such height
As, but in thee, was ne'r exprest;

Brave wormes, and Earth! that thus could have
A God Enclos'd within your Cell,
Your maker pent up in a grave,
Life lockt in death, heav'n in a shell;

Ah, my deare Lord! what couldst thou spye
In this impure, rebellious clay,
That made thee thus resolve to dye
For those that kill thee every day?

O what strange wonders could thee move
To slight thy precious bloud, and breath!
Sure it was *Love,* my Lord; for *Love*
Is only stronger far than death.

Henry Vaughan
(c. 1621-1695)

The Lord has sent me
to bring good news to the poor.
Christmas is the feast of the poor—
a very poor feast,
the birth of a child
who was rejected by everyone.
And the first to come to the crib
were simple people—
shepherds, poor people.
They were the first
to hear the good news
and to be told:
"Today the Savior is born for you."

Jean Vanier
(Founder of the Arche Centers
for the Handicapped, b. 1929)

How I admire the Lord,
the Creator of the world!
He wanted to be born
not surrounded by gold and silver,
but just on a piece of this earth.

Saint Jerome
(Latin Church Father, d. 420)

I myself am very glad that the divine child was born in a stable, because my soul is very much like a stable, filled with strange unsatisfied longings, with guilt and animal-like impulses, tormented by anxiety, inadequacy and pain. If the holy One could be born in such a place, the One can be born in me also. I am not excluded.

Morton Kelsey

You are with us, Emmanuel.
You are with us as a human being,
as a new-born child,
weak and vulnerable,
wrapped in swaddling cloths
and lying in a crib
"because there was no place for them
at the inn."
Could you ever have done any more
than you did
to be our Emmanuel, God with us?

Pope John Paul II
(b. 1920)

The stable of Jesus' birth reminds us that he is a very different kind of king—one born in poverty, one who comes to serve and not to be served. It is this kind of Messiah we are called to follow—to serve others, be light for others. And we take comfort and courage in the belief that Jesus is "Emmanuel"—"God with us"—to guide our feet into the path of peace.

James McGinnis

Jesus,
what made you so small?
Love!

Bernard of Clairvaux
(1090-1153)

* * *

Since this holy night
God has been in this world
and the world has been in God.

Odo Casel
(1886-1948)

This is the month, and this the happy morn
Wherein the Son of Heav'n's eternal King,
Of wedded maid, and virgin mother born,
Our great redemption from above did bring;
For so the holy sages once did sing,
That he our deadly forfeit should release,
And with his Father work us a perpetual
    peace.

That glorious form, that light insufferable,
And that far-beaming blaze of majesty,
Wherewith he wont at Heav'n's high
    council-table
To sit the midst of Trinal Unity,
He laid aside; and here with us to be,
Forsook the courts of everlasting day,
And chose with us a darksome house of
    mortal clay.

Say Heav'nly Muse, shall not thy sacred vein
Afford a present to the Infant God?
Hast thou no verse, no hymn, or solemn
    strain,
To welcome him to this his new abode,
Now while the heav'n by the sun's team
    untrod,
Hath took no print of the approaching light,
And all the spangled host keep watch in
    squadrons bright?

See how from far upon the eastern road
The star-led Wisards haste with odors sweet,
O run, prevent them with thy humble ode,
And lay it lowly at his blessed feet;
Have thou the honor first, thy Lord to greet,
And join thy voice unto the angel quire,
From out his secret altar toucht with
  hallow'd fire.

John Milton
(1608-1674)

When the King of Kings was born,
he chose his parents
from among the little people of this world.
And the simple people of the district
were the first he invited to his cradle—
those who slept under the stars of heaven
and could hear the angel's voice.
It was only then
that he received the great ones of the world.
They were also his children,
but their lives were threatened
by glory and honor.
He called them,
but they were so far off
that the journey took them a long time.
Those mighty kings announced their arrival
with expensive presents.
But first they kneeled down—
humility was their real gift.
They kneeled down
after the shepherds.
That is how Christmas was
and that is how it will be
until the end of the world.

Gilbert Cesbron
(French author, b. 1913)

A light has come from Bethlehem
that has continued to enlighten
the hearts of men and women.
The angels' message
again and again gives us new hope.
Centuries have passed since then
and so much has happened
to make us lose heart—
wars and disasters
and disappointments of every kind.
But that good news,
the grace of that child
and the happiness of that mother
have continued to help people and nations
to free themselves from the night
in which they again and again
have found themselves straying.

Igino Giordani
(Italian author, 1894-1980)

God became a child
in order to tell us
that he is not far away.
The angels are singing:
"Peace to people on earth."
We ask him,
who became defenseless
that he will extinguish in us
the flame of the pride of power
and take hatred out of our hearts,
filling them with love,
so that it will not be long
before no nation in the world
will remember what war is.

Chiara Lubich (b. 1920)

When peaceful stillness composed
   everything
and the night in its swift course was half spent
your all-powerful word from heaven's royal
   throne,
bounded, a fierce warrior into the doomed land,
bearing the sharp sword
of your inexorable decree.

Wisdom 18:14-16a

36

Were my eyes to see you come down,
they would cease to weep.
Rain him down, you clouds—
the one whom earth has longed for.

Earth, you have given us only thorns.
Be open now and bring forth
the only flower
in which you yourself may flourish.

John of the Cross
(1542-1591)

How much you have loved us,
kind Father!
If your Word had not become flesh
and had not dwelt among us,
we would have had to believe
that there was no connection
between God and humanity
and we would have been in despair.

Augustine
(Bishop of Hippo, d. 430)

With Jesus a new humanity was born, consisting of heaven and earth, of the visible and the invisible and of human and divine hope. It is composed of members who are citizens both of heaven and of earth, human children and children of God. In his power, every human being can be the son or daughter of the most high God and the dwelling place of God on earth and every man and woman can inherit heaven.

The Word became flesh. God became human and human beings were able to look at God on this earth. If Jesus is really God who became human, then something is bound to have changed fundamentally in human history. If God really entered our history, then that history must have been placed under a new sign.

When God became human, humanity became "God's space" and men and women became related to God and Christ's brothers and sisters. If God became one of us in Jesus, that is surely something that we can never value highly enough. We can place all our human hopes on him. If Jesus is at the same time both God and our brother, then I should never know fear again.

God is my brother. This reveals new horizons to us and changes our whole existence. Our measures have changed—the kingdom of God is above all immeasurable. We inherit God. With all our sins, we are saints!

Carlo Carretto
(1910-1988)

38

The one who embraces everything
and who created everything
came into the world
like every other person!
We hear the one at whose word
the angels and archangels tremble
cry like a child.
He did not need to become human,
because we humans were created by him,
but we needed
God to become flesh
and dwell among us.
His lowliness is our distinction
and his ignominy is our honor.
What he continues to be,
by becoming flesh as God,
we become,
renewed from the flesh into God.

Hilary
(Bishop of Poitiers, d. 367)

Christmas, a season of paradox, when the topsy-turvy logic of the divine becomes most evident: the Infinite shut in the finite, the Almighty reduced to a powerless babe, the Light and Life of All Ages bursting into history in the dark dead of winter.

Is this not the work of love—love which seeks always to become the other, and in becoming that which is other than itself affirms itself as love? Is it not a prefiguring of the climax of love on this earth, in the death of Jesus on the cross when love became nothing, taking non-love on itself and becoming sin? Christmas and the paschal mystery both shout out that love in losing itself is itself, utterly itself.

And both moments show us the pathway of love, the secret of God's own inner life which we all can share.

Charles Wheatley
(b. 1955)

God's becoming human
is not an idyll.
It is a scandal!
God meets us
in the lowliness of a child.

Klaus Hemmerle
(Bishop of Aachen, Germany)

When the time had come
that God had previously chosen
for the redemption of humankind,
his Son, Jesus Christ
lodged on our lowly earth.
He, the incomprehensible one,
wanted to be grasped.
He who was before all time
took his beginning in time.
He who was invisible in his being
became visible in our flesh.
The God who was incapable of suffering
was not ashamed to be
a human being capable of suffering.
The God who was immortal
submitted himself to the law of death.

Leo the Great
(Pope, d. 461)

You wanted to be God,
although you were human
and so you were lost.
He wanted to be human,
although he was God,
so that he could look for what was lost.
Your human pride
struck you down with such force
that only the humility of God
could make you rise up again.

Augustine
(Bishop of Hippo, d. 430)

God's Son became human
so that human beings
might have their home in God.

Hildegard of Bingen
(1098-1179)

The one who has from eternity
been in the bosom of the Father
is now resting on his mother's knees.
God is so close to you
that he lets himself be embraced like a child
and held like a baby at the breast—
for "the Word became flesh
and dwelt among us."
How is it possible for him
to be more like you
and more closely related to you?
Look, he has your flesh and bones!
God has become your brother.

Thomas à Kempis
(1379/80-1471)

44

Jesus comes back into the world
when we offer him a dwelling-place in our
   hearts,
when we accept him in his law of love,
when we do what Mary did
and conceive Jesus and carry him in us,
so that he is able to become
the heart of our life.
Then he will love the heavenly Father
with our whole heart,
with our whole soul
and with all our strength.
Then his love and goodness
and his sympathy for all men and women
will shine out into the world
like a light through us.
Then he will smile through our eyes
and help with our hands
and once again live
his redeeming life of the Gospel.
Then we shall be the doors,
the tens and hundreds of thousands of doors,
through which he, the Lord,
the Prince of Peace,
God-with-us, will enter
his world, his kingdom.

   Werenfried van Straaten

The new world order is this—
God lets himself be so influenced
by his love for his image and likeness
that he becomes a little baby.
He lets himself be laid in a crib
to show that he will be
both shepherd and pasture for his people.
He, who is eternity without ageing,
subjects himself to the human law
of becoming older.
Although he is God,
he takes all suffering onto himself
like a weak human being.
He does this
to put an end to the law of death
and to enable us to share in immortality.
God's power is this:
that he can be what he is not
and yet still remain what he is.
He is our God—
the eternal Son of the eternal Father.
He is God and he is human,
because he stands in the middle,
between the Father and us.
The reality of his flesh is revealed
in his weakness
and the reality of his majesty is revealed
in his miracles.

Zeno (Bishop of Verona, d. 371/72)

God fulfilled the promises that he had made to his prophets and gave his people what they had been longing for, but everything turned out differently from what they had expected. God's thoughts are always quite different from human thoughts. They seem at first to fall short of our expectations, but in fact they go far beyond them—as far as heaven is from our earth.

God came on earth as a human being and first revealed his human love in the human face of a little child. He did not come in terrible majesty, in overwhelming light or in visible power and glory. He came in weakness and impotence. He almost came secretly. He was even despised and rejected. He did not come to display his omnipotence, to make wisdom shine on the world, to judge evil or to help justice to be victorious. That was not his way of establishing a kingdom of God on earth. No, he came to reveal God's *agape* in other words, that self-giving, sacrificial love that is only present in God.

That is the sublime wisdom of the mystery of Christianity—that God is *agape* and that his *agape* shone on us in a human face, the face of the kindest, most selfless and most loving of all human beings.

Odo Casel
(1886-1948)

Flocks feed by darkness with a noise of
   whispers
In the dry grass of pastures,
And lull the solemn night with their weak bells.

The little towns upon the rocky hills
Look down as meek as children:
Because they have seen come this holy time.

God's glory, now, is kindled gentler than low
   candlelight
Under the rafters of a barn:
Eternal Peace is sleeping in the hay,
And Wisdom's born in secret in a straw-roofed
   stable.

And O! Make holy music in the stars, you happy
   angels.
You shepherds, gather on the hill.
Look up, you timed flocks, where the three kings
Are coming through the wintry trees;

While we unnumbered children of the wicked
   centuries
Come after with our penances and prayers,
And lay them down in the sweet-smelling hay
Beside the wise men's golden jars.

Thomas Merton

The birthday of the Lord
is the birthday of peace.

The birth of Christ
is the origin of the Christian people
and the birthday of the head
is also the birthday of the body.

Leo the Great
(Pope, d. 461)

Christmas.
Heaven has opened its gates.
The Word has become flesh
and has brought
the fire of love
to earth.

Because we do not want
this day ever to end,
we ask you, Lord,
that we may love one another
as you loved us
and we ask you
to stay among us,
present in our midst.

In that way every day
could be Christmas day for us.

Chiara Lubich
(b. 1920)

Christmas!
On that night
was born in a manger the poor man
whose love was to shake the world.

Christmas!
Since that time no one has the right
to be happy in isolation.

Raoul Follereau
(1903-1977)

Anyone who has really understood
that God became human
can never speak and act
in an inhuman way.

Karl Barth
(1886-1968)

We are not just promised freedom—
we have it already.
It is not a present in the future—
it has been given to us.
It has not simply been predicted—
it is present here and now.
For with the fullness of time
came the fullness of God.

Where else does such great love exist?
Today we can understand
the depth of God's concern for us.
Today we can experience
what he thinks of us.

Bernard of Clairvaux
(1090-1153)

He is simply there—
that is all
that he does
or that he can do.
But, by being there,
powerless yet radiant,
it is God himself
who is there.
God is there for us.
What, then, does this being God
in the child of Bethlehem
say to us?
It says to me and to you
and to every human being:
it is good that you are there.

Klaus Hemmerle
(Bishop of Aachen, Germany)

What suitable response can we make
to such a great honor—
the honor that you have bestowed on us
by giving us such great love?
God's only Son,
whose divine origin
is beyond description,
entered the womb of the holy Virgin
and assumed the form of a human being.
He, who holds everything in being
and in whom and for whom everything exists,
was born in harmony
with the laws of human nature.
The one, at whose voice
angels and archangels tremble
and heaven and earth
and all the elements of this world melt away,
the unseen one,
who does not let himself
be confined to any human reality,
whom we can neither touch, nor feel, nor hold—
we see him in a crib,
wrapped in swaddling cloths.
Anyone who thinks about these things
that are so unworthy of God
will be all the more strongly
convinced of his love.
For him, by whose will we were created,
it was, after all, not necessary

to become human.
But it was for us
that he assumed human nature
and wanted to live among us.
His humility
is our great dignity.
God was born as a human being!
Or, to look at it
from another point of view,
we were reborn in God.

Hilary
(Bishop of Poitiers, d. 367)

When Jesus was born,
full of joy the angels announced his coming:
"Rejoice!"
Joy, because Jesus is born.
The shepherds and all those who had gathered
around Jesus, seemed to emanate joy.
That same joy, which Jesus came to bring as he
himself told us.

A heart full of joy
is like a ray of God's love,
hope for everlasting happiness,
a burning, divine fire.
If we make room for Jesus
to live within us
we will experience this joy.
And when we pray, we too become
a fountain of the love of God—
in our homes, where we live
and ultimately for the whole world.

Mother Teresa of Calcutta

God is the Lord
and he appeared to us.
He came, not in the form of God,
so that he would not frighten the weak,
but in the form of a servant,
so that he could lead the enslaved to freedom.
Is there anyone
who is so weary
or so ungrateful
not to be overjoyed
at this day?

Basil the Great
(Bishop of Caesarea, d. 379)

Long before we had any hope in ourselves, God had great hope and confidence in us. Long before we had a chance to make up our own dreams, God had a dream bigger and better than anything we could imagine for ourselves. How do we know this?

The feast of Christmas tells us. We read in Saint John's gospel that "God so loved the world that he sent his only son that we might not perish but have everlasting life." In other words, God had so much confidence and hope in us that he gave us the gift of his Son. God has put his Son into our hands. And that is the ultimate sign of his confidence, trust, and hope in us. He has let us hold his Son as a little baby, so great is his trust and hope in us.

Joseph Cardinal Bernardin
(in an address to prisoners)

Jesus did not come exclusively
for people with white skin,
nor did he come only for black people.
He did not come simply for Europeans
or just for people in other parts of the world.
Christ became human
for the whole of humankind.
That means
he also came for each one of us.
It also means
a feast for all of us,
joy for all of us
and freedom and peace
for all of us.

Chiara Lubich
(b. 1920)

Gold, friend, power and honor—
nothing can make us so happy
as the joyful news
that Christ became man.
The human heart can scarcely conceive it
and we can certainly not talk enough about it.
To do such a thing
and let us hear about it,
God must love us with all his heart.
He must love me
because he comes so close to me,
because he became human with me.
He became
what I am.

Martin Luther
(1483-1546)

61

God, the Lord, has made his mercy known—
his song has sounded in the night.

This is the day that the Lord has made—
let us be glad and rejoice in it!

The dear and holy child has been given to us
as our companion on the way.

He was born in a manger—
there was no place in the inn.

Glory to God in the highest
and peace on earth among people of good will!

May the heavens rejoice
and the earth shout with joy!
Let the sea exult and all that it surrounds!
let the fields be glad
and all that grows in them!

Sing a new song to the Lord—
let every land sing to the Lord!

For the Lord is great and worthy of our praise,
greater than all other gods.

All nations, praise the Lord,
and all the people of the earth, praise him!
Honor the name of the Lord!

Francis of Assisi (1181/2-1226)

God's Son became a human being.
All our efforts to understand
this great mystery are in vain.
All that we can do
is what the shepherds did—
worship, believe and praise God.

Cardinal Alfred Bengsch
(1921-1979)

The shepherds sing; and shall I silent be?
   My God, no hymn for Thee?
My soul's a shepherd too; a flock it feeds
   Of thoughts, and words, and deeds.
The pasture is Thy Word; the streams Thy grace,
   Enriching all the place.
Shepherd and flock shall sing, and all my
         powers
   Outsing the daylight hours;
Then we will chide the sun for letting night
   Take up his place and right;
We sing one common Lord; wherefore He
         should
Himself the candle hold.

George Herbert
(1593-1633)

Who could doubt the greatness of this event—that the exalted ruler of the world should come down from such a great distance to a place that was so unworthy? Why, then, did he come down? We know why, because what he actually said and did tell us clearly the reason for his coming. He hurried down from the mountains to look among the hundreds of sheep for the one that had gone astray. He came for our sake, so that his mercy and his wonderful deeds would proclaim to the human race even more visibly the praise of the Lord.

How wonderful is the condescension of the God who seeks us and how great is the dignity of those who are sought by him! All the wealth and all the glory of the world and everything that is desirable in the world—none of this means so much as this great honor. Nothing can be compared with it. Lord, what is the human race, that you have made it so great? Why are you so attached to it?

It would have been more appropriate, surely, if we had come to him. But two things prevented us from doing that. Our eyes were clouded and he dwells in inaccessible light. And we were crippled and could not come to him. That is why he came to us—he, the physician of our souls.

Bernard of Clairvaux
(1090-1153)

The middle of the night
is the beginning of the day.
The middle of need
is the beginning of the light.

From an old carol

Among the oxen (like an ox I'm slow)
I see a glory in the stable grow
Which, with the ox's dullness might at length
Give me an ox's strength.

Among the asses (stubborn I as they)
I see my Savior where I looked for hay;
So may my beastlike folly learn at least
The patience of a beast.

Among the sheep (I like a sheep have strayed)
I watch the manger where my Lord is laid;
Oh that my baa-ing nature would win thence
Some woolly innocence.

C.S. Lewis

The light that shines in the darkness
is in no sense abstract,
nor is it just ordinary.
It is not simply a demand imposed on us
to be good to each other.
No, it is something
that is both living and personal.
It is Jesus Christ,
Mary's son and the Son of God.
Mary was the first to understand
that her life had been given
an entirely new meaning
and that, in this child,
the life of the whole of humanity
had been made new.

Carlo Maria Martini
(Archbishop of Milan)

Praise to the holy Trinity,
who decided
that human dignity should be restored
and that the devil's cunning
should be put to shame.
I praise you, heavenly Father,
who sent your beloved Son
into this world
to redeem us.
I praise you,
Son of God, Jesus Christ,
who assumed our nature
in order to redeem us human beings.
I praise you, Comforter, Holy Spirit,
who, from the beginning to the end,
have wonderfully and gloriously carried out
all the saving acts of our redemption.
Praise, glory, honor and blessing
be yours, most exalted Trinity,
the origin and the beginning
of our feast today
and the source of our joy!

Thomas à Kempis
(1379/80-1471)

Christmas is our feast.

Today we celebrate God's coming to us so that we might return to him, taking off the old nature and putting on the new. As we died in Adam, so we shall live in Christ, by being born with him, crucified with him and rising again with him.

Be glad about his conception and leap, perhaps not like John the Baptist in his mother's womb, but certainly like David, when the ark of the covenant reached its resting place.

Honor the enrolment, by which you have been enrolled for heaven.

Celebrate the birth, by which you have been redeemed.

Respect little Bethlehem, which has brought you back to paradise.

Revere the crib, by which you were nourished by the Word, after having lost knowledge.

Follow the star and with the wise men offer gifts to him who died for you.

Praise him with the shepherds, sing joyful songs with the angels and dance with the archangels.

Together let us celebrate the feast in heaven and on earth, for I am certain that those who are in heaven are also rejoicing, because they love the God-man.

Gregory Nazianzen
(330-390)

The human race was made God's likeness,
but, since we lost that form,
God took our human likeness
this night, when he was born.

Andreas Gryphius
(1616-1664)

The day of our dear Redeemer's birth
is the day that opened to us
the door of everlasting life.

Elizabeth Ann Seton

The eternal Word was born, here and this day.
And where was that? Where you yourself did
  stray.

Though heaven sink down, the earth to fructify,
when will the earth rise up to meet the sky?

Were Christ a thousand times in Bethlehem
  born
and not in you, you would remain forlorn.

So open wide your heart and let God in,
you should his kingdom be and he your king.

When God begot his first-born Son on earth,
he called us to assist the wondrous birth.

What good is Mary's greeting, Gabriel,
if you be not my messenger as well?

Angelus Silesius
(1624-1677)

All praises to you, Christ our Lord,
that you were born a human child,
born of a maiden undefiled
whom angel hosts sing and applaud.

The eternal Father's only child,
he who is everlasting good,
clothed in our flesh and our poor blood,
lives in a stable bleak and wild.

The world could not contain in space
him who, confined in Mary's womb,
has now become a little one,
yet holds the world in his embrace.

Eternal glory shines so bright
and so transforms this world of sin,
it shines in midnight dark and dim
and makes us children of the light.

So poor on earth is his estate
that he might pity our distress
and make us rich in heavenly grace
and equal to the angels' state.

All this for us he freely bore
to show his love for humankind.
All Christendom rejoice in mind
and thank our Savior evermore!

Martin Luther (1483-1546)

What is Christmas?

It is the most interesting story
that has ever been told.

Charles Péguy
(1873-1914)

Our Redeemer was born today,
so we must celebrate with festive joy.
We cannot be sad today
because it is the Lord's birthday.
The saint rejoices
because he is close
to the victor's palm
and the sinner is glad
because forgiveness
will soon be his.
The pagan can breathe in peace
because he is called to life.

Leo the Great
(Pope, d. 461)

When we look for you within ourselves,
when we worship you in the form of bread,
when we speak with you, the Lord of the world,
when we thank you for our lives,
when we offer you the pain caused by
our mistakes
and ask you to help us—
we always see you as an adult.
But every year at Christmas,
you reveal yourself to us
as a child born in a crib.
We stand in silent amazement
and do not know what to ask.
We do not want to be a nuisance to you,
for, although you are omnipotent,
you show yourself as a child.

In silent adoration we stand before the mystery,
like Mary when the shepherds came
and told her what they had seen and heard:
"She kept all these things,
pondering them in her heart."

Christmas:
Again and again the Child appears to us
as one of the most profound mysteries of faith
and as the first sign of that love for us
that will be made manifest
in the fullness of God's mercy and omnipotence.

Chiara Lubich (b.1920)

Child, dear child,
help me to discover
even in the most earnest
and the most severe people
the child asleep in their hearts.

*   *   *

Mary, full of grace,
your son was born
but you continue to be pregnant,
full of grace,
full of God.

*   *   *

In the vigil
that we keep again tonight
to celebrate
the Word's becoming human,
there is the prayer
that has proved to be
the most valuable of all—
silence.

Dom Helder Camara
(b. 1909)

Christ,
we thank you
that we are able to achieve something,
even though we are so fragile.

We praise you, Jesus Christ,
because you know
how helpless we are
and yet continue to come
to sing in us
the joyful song
of unshakable trust.

Brother Roger Schutz
(Taizé)

Like a mother rejoicing over her new born
   baby,
like a child rejoicing over his little brother,
like a bride rejoicing over her bridegroom—
the Church rejoices over Christ,
who brings fulfillment to everyone.
The Church sings with joy on this holy night
because the Son of God was born.
He is our life.
He knows our poverty and our sadness
and our hopes and desires.

Carlo Maria Martini
(Archbishop of Milan, b. 1927)

In the crib, Jesus radiates
what the world so much needs today—
gentleness, tenderness, light and hope.

Gentleness—as the answer to all violence.
Tenderness—as the answer to the lack of
    goodness,
benevolence and love of our brothers and sisters
(even among those who call themselves
    Christians).
Light—as the answer to the shadows that darken
the present time.
Hope—as the answer to those who feel
    abandoned
or who find no meaning in their lives.

Little Sister Magdeleine of Jesus
(Founder of the Little Sisters of Jesus,
1898-1989)

Christmas means:
He has come.
He has made the night clear.
He has made the night of our darkness,
the night of our lack of understanding,
the cruel night
of our fears
and our hopelessness
into Christmas, the holy night.

In the Word made flesh,
God has sent his last Word,
his most profound Word,
his most beautiful Word
into the world.
And that Word means:
I love you,
world and humanity.
Light the candles!
They have more right here
than darkness.

Karl Rahner

The world has continued on its course, but it has become the ship of God that no storm can overturn and no current can deflect. Life has continued to obey its laws and to respond to its tensions, but God has subjected himself to those tensions and has fitted himself into them. He now shares them with us and has in this way raised what the whole of humanity is capable of being and doing to a higher level.

We are no longer alone as human beings. We have never been able to live happily and healthily simply on the basis of monologue. It is only in dialogue that we can live sound, full and authentic lives. Every movement towards monologue is evil. But the existence of tensions in God's being and in his burdens is now calling us to share in dialogue with him and that is his way of finally and forever overcoming the most terrible of human illnesses—loneliness. There is now no night that is without light. There is no prison cell without some authentic conversation. There is no lonely mountain path or dangerous descent into the abyss without someone to accompany and lead us.

God is with us. That was his promise and we have wept and beseeched him. And that promise has become a reality in our lives, in quite a different way from what we expected, a much fuller and much simpler reality than we had thought it would be.

We should not try to avoid God's burdens. They

are the way to his blessing. If we continue faithfully to follow the hard way, bearing God's burdens, we shall discover the inner source of reality and the world will reveal itself as being not silent in a sense that is quite different from what we had imagined. The silver threads of the divine mystery of all reality will begin to gleam and sing aloud for us. Those burdens will become a blessing for us, as soon as we recognize them and bear them as God's burdens.

God became human. We did not become God. The human dispensation continues and it must continue. But it is consecrated. And we have become more. We have also been strengthened. Let us trust our life, then, because this night has brought us light. Let us trust life, because we do not live it alone. God lives it with us.

Alfred Delp, S.J.
(condemned to death in Germany
on February 2, 1945)

The true meaning of Christmas
is not to be found exclusively
in the love of hearth and home,
the happiness of children
or the family gathering.
It can also be celebrated
by those who are lonely,
who are separated from their family
or who simply have no family.
Christmas is not just the feast
of those who have something to give—
it is also the feast
of those who have nothing to give
or no one to give to.
It is not only a family feast—
it is also the feast of those who are alone.

Romano Guardini
(1885-1968)

The Redeemer who was born in Bethlehem
is not a distant and anonymous God.
He is the "God with us"
who has counted every hair on our heads.
He accompanies each one of us
throughout our lives
and he has accompanied all of us
throughout the whole of our history.
He is looking for inner fellowship with us.

Patriarch Athenagoras
(1886-1972)

Whatis the real meaning of our giving at Christmas? Christmas presents are not given universally by every nation and culture in the world. Why is it, then, that, unlike other people, we have, since time immemorial, made Christmas the feast of giving? Many different answers could be given to this question by those who specialize in social history or the philosophy of religion, many of them very helpful and edifying. But I would like to ignore scholarship for the moment and suggest that we just question our own hearts.

We may be poor or we may be well off, but all of us will have spent time before Christmas looking for and buying something to give to those we love. We may have spent hours thinking about an unusual gift for someone. Or we may have wanted to surprise the person who receives our present. It may have cost us more money than we could really afford. And one of the happiest experiences in the world is when we look forward with the eager expectation of a child to a Christmas present or the surprise that we feel—or pretend, with a rather painful smile, to feel—when the packages lying under the Christmas tree are unwrapped. What is revealed in all this is a deep human longing.

In every one of us, there is hidden, somewhere in the depths of our being, a poet or an artist who is prevented from expressing himself or herself by the everyday tasks. As Baudelaire said, our heart is like a captive albatross on the deck of the ship of life—an awkward, incongruous, ridiculous creature when not in the sky, because it is made for flight and its huge wings prevent it from walking.

We are men and women and we have many very ordinary tasks and duties to do in the hustle and bustle of our lives. On grey days we very often think of them as "wretched hateful jobs." But our human experience ought really to be different from this. This hustle and bustle ought to be more loving and touch our hearts more closely, but it only leaves us time and money for those ordinary tasks and duties and for what is strictly necessary. It does not touch our hearts at all, but leaves them poor and empty. Goodness withers away in us and so does love, which can only flourish in a unique situation, when everything is in abundance—in a word, when there is a feast.

What happens in the weeks before Christmas? They are weeks of thinking, planning and preparation. The little girl may begin in secret to knit or sew something for her parents. The young man tries to find out, without asking, what kind of gift will really please the girl he loves. Mother may be using all her ingenuity to conjure up happiness from nothing and father may become a boy again and try to put the old model railway in running order or even make some toys himself. And the children, those people who are still wise and not yet disappointed by life's experiences—they feel safe and happy in the care of their parents. Every parent is, after all, the representative of the infinitely rich Christ child.

This is also where we find the deeper metaphysical meaning of the long-established tradition of giving special presents at Christmas, the practice of wanting to give much more than we are able to give or can afford to give. When we go beyond our resources and ability in this way, we become aware that there is something that transcends our ordinary everyday tasks and duties, something that gives us an insight into the nature of the kingdom of God, in which all of us are rich, generous in giving and indeed almost as almighty as God himself.

Every gift is . . . a symbol of our love. Every present is like a sacramental, a making visible of an invisible good that goes further than our calculations, has no boundaries and recognizes no frontiers. And however poor we may be, so poor that we have, in the weeks before Christmas, to go past the shop windows and their glorious displays of gifts perhaps with a troubled, hurt and even envious heart, we can still say on Christmas day to those we love: I give you my heart. My heart, my loving heart, is like a carefully locked Christmas present. It contains treasures that have still not been discovered. My love is new and full of surprises. It looks forward to receiving a gift in return. And it is renewed and made young again when it hears the only possible answer: I love you too.

Hugo Rahner
(1900-1968)

The Word became flesh
the hidden became visible,
the uncreated entered creation
and light shone in the darkness.
Everything else came from this—
the candles, the colors, the gifts,
the good wishes and the carols.
But Christmas is not just that alone.
What this unique Christian feast aims to do
is to give us a deep conviction
and a firm faith in one great truth:
When God came down
from heaven to earth for us
he did so because he loves us.
When someone loves us,
life becomes easier for us
and we can understand everything more clearly.
We can detect that person's hand
behind the shadow of our existence.
We often do not know why, but we know
that person's love lies behind everything.
Our burdens become lighter
and good experiences become quite joyful.
Life is no longer just a bare outline
because love is in flower behind it,
a child is born
and we are surprised
by unexpected happiness.
We know a loving Father is caring for us.

When we believe in a God who loves us,
everything becomes possible,
even if it seems impossible,
like the apparent impossibility
of peace on our earth.

The almighty one came to us
and because of this
our faith can never be too strong.
We can be sure
that our world is moving
in the direction of unity
and we pray with all our heart
that nations and peoples,
societies and generations,
religions and churches
and people of every generation
will come closer and closer to one another.
This movement towards unity
is something that characterizes
the age we are living in.
Many young people believe in this aim
and are committed to achieving it.
The child whose birth we celebrate today
was not less committed to this dream.
He came into the world
so that we should be one
and he laid down his life
so that this dream should become a reality.

Chiara Lubich (b. 1920)

Gloria Deo et pax hominibus—these words are over the new-born Savior. But they were only reached after Joseph, Mary and the Child had followed the way of countless disappointments, discomforts, adversities and unpleasant experiences. From the human point of view, everything should have been quite different, but the Savior wanted it to be like this and chose this way. He did so to be an example for us—almost a motto, under which we could give glory to God and bring peace to our fellow people. A motto for us and for me!

My present life is so comfortable and so easy. So I have to stir myself and accept the adversities and unpleasant experiences that my work brings, accept them in imitation of my Savior, just as Mary and Joseph accepted them in the same spirit.

From the diary of Cardinal Augustin Bea
(1881-1968)

The divine child
fulfills the promise.
It is only where he is awaited
that he is received.
Otherwise no child
is born for us tonight.
But where he is accepted
he exceeds every expectation.

Jean-Marie Lustiger
(Archbishop of Paris, b. 1926)

Since Bethlehem,
our earth has been changed for ever.
Since then, it has borne God's glory.

Since then,
no power has ever been able
to tear this earth out of God's hands.

Cardinal Alfred Bengsch
(1921-1979)

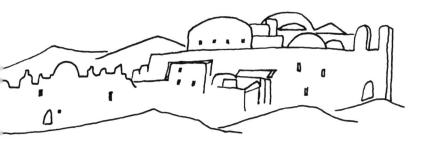

We desire to be able to welcome Jesus
at Christmas time,
not in a cold manger of our heart
but in a heart full of love and humility,
in a heart so pure,
so immaculate,
so warm with love for one another.

Mother Teresa of Calcutta
(b.1910)

What is Christmas?
It is living in hope,
holding out the hand of reconciliation,
accepting strangers,
helping one another to do good,
wiping away tears.

Every time love is given,
distress is relieved
and someone is made happy,
God comes down from heaven
and brings us light.
That is Christmas.

A carol from Haiti

We are on the way to you . . .

From the villages and towns,
from the hills and valleys,
with suffering brothers and sisters,
with laughing children.
as builders of peace,
as messengers of justice,
as witnesses to your love,
as members of your Church . . .

. . . we are on the way to you.

When we support the weak,
when we pray for the persecuted,
we are on the way to you.

When we celebrate your presence,
you are with your people.

From a Latin American hymn

Lord,

we pray for the people
who are far from you,
for it is above all for them
that you came into the world
on that day.

Chiara Lubich
(b.1920)

This Christmas I pray
for myself,
for all my sisters and brothers,
for all men and women of good will,
for those who are burdened with cares
and for those who are seeking.

Help us,
so that we may see God's smile
in the face of a child.
Give us a new heart,
so that we may receive the divine child,
understand his message
and bear it in our everyday lives.
Give us the strength
to accompany the Lord
throughout the year ahead
and to follow in his footsteps.

Cardinal Léon-Joseph Suenens
(b. 1904)

The star of Bethlehem
is a star in the darkness of night
even today.

Edith Stein
(1891-1942)

Our rich world
has claimed Christmas for itself
and has thrust Jesus outside.
Christmas has become a poetic fantasy,
a friendly atmosphere,
an exchange of gifts,
a symbol of light, stars and carols,
a boom in the sale of luxury goods.
And who thinks of Jesus?
He came to his own home,
but his own people did not receive him.
There was no place for him in the inn—
not even at Christmas.
I would so much like to found a business
that would publicize the real meaning of
    Christmas.

I would like to print the most beautiful cards
and have the most impressive figures made.
I would write poems,
collect old and new carols,
illustrate books for children and grown-ups
and write scripts for films and plays.
It is hurtful to experience the way
people cling to Christmas as a season
but reject the child born at Christmas.
So we must at least let it be seen in our homes
who was born on Christmas day
and let us prepare for him
the best feast we have ever prepared.

Chiara Lubich (b. 1920)

Christmas
is the last word
pronounced over us.
It tells us
that we are loved,
that we are free
and that we are able
to follow the way to God,
that we are new-born
and can begin again our life
and our work of building up society.
This word of hope
lies behind all the greetings
that we send to each other
at Christmas.
It is the true meaning
of all the presents
that we send to each other.
The child who comes to us
is the sign given to us
that God has opened the door
that leads to this way.

Carlo Maria Martini
(Archbishop of Milan, b. 1927)

Author's Index